Covenant Bible Study Series

The Life of David

by Larry Fourman

Brethren Press
Elgin, Illinois

Covenant Bible Study Series
Life of David

Brethren Press, 1451 Dundee Avenue, Elgin, IL 60120

Cover design by Jeane Healy

Library of Congress Cataloging-in-Publication Data

Fourman, Larry.
The life of David / Larry Fourman ; foreword by June Adams Gibble.
p. cm.
ISBN 0-87178-518-8
1. David, King of Israel. 2. Bible. O.T.—Biography. 3. Bible. O.T. Samuel—Study. 4. Bible. O.T. Kings, 1st—Study. I. Title.
BS580.D3F65 1990
222'.4092—dc20
[B] 90-39039
CIP

Manufactured in the United States of America

Contents

Foreword

A warm memory from my early years is hearing my dad singing "Little David, play on your harp, hallelu, hallelu, little David, play on your harp....Little David was a shepherd boy..." and on the song went. How easy it was, through a child's eyes, to "see" the story of this long-ago shepherd boy who became a king.

Most of us have such memories, recalled from early home and family life or from Sunday School settings. We heard David's stories and we memorized David's psalms. As we grew older, we learned more about David's life, including the many complexities of his family life, political life, and religious life. Perhaps at times we have recognized in David's life some of the same complexities that confront our own lives.

This Bible study, "The Life of David," presents an overview of David's life, from his youth until his death. We see David's fears and hopes, his failures and accomplishments. We follow his struggles to faithfully live out covenants made with himself, with other people, and with God. And as we follow his story, we are led into a deeper look at our own life. Where are our struggles and failures, our hopes and accomplishments similar to those of David? How do we live out commitments and covenants in ways that reflect maturing faith and faithfulness? How do we experience God moving surely and steadfastly in our lives?

This relational Bible study is designed for small group settings within the congregation. As you begin to study "The Life of David," you will want to keep in mind some ways in which relational Bible study differs from other kinds of Bible study.

It is important to recognize that relational Bible study has strong biblical foundations. It is anchored in the covenantal history of God's people; it recognizes that God made covenant with a people and lived in relationship to that people. And it recognizes that God's empowerment comes to the community today as persons gather to pray and to study, to share and to receive, to reflect and to act. The gathered community is necessary for growing up in faith. Such growth does not just happen—it must be struggled for in the power of the Holy Spirit and in accord with the teachings of Jesus.

Relational Bible study takes seriously the corporateness of the faith. The Body of Christ becomes a reality within the life of the group, as each person contributes to the group's study, prayer, and work together. Each one's contribution is needed as the group seeks the meaning of the text. "For just as the body is one and has many members, and all the members of the body, though many, are one body, so it is with Christ....Now you are the body of Christ and individually members of it" (1 Cor. 12:12, 17).

Relational Bible study helps both persons and the group to claim the promise of the Spirit, to be open to the active working of the Holy Spirit in their midst. This kind of small group life and study knows that "...where two or three have met together in my name, I am there among them" (Matt. 18:20).

Building upon these understandings of relational Bible study, your group will want to give careful attention to these guidelines:

1. As a small group of learners, we gather around God's Word to discern God's word for us today.
2. The words, stories, and admonitions we find in scripture come alive for us today and relate to the lives we live today.
3. All persons are learners and all are leaders; we all come needing to learn, and we all come to "lead," to teach.
4. Each person will contribute to the study, sharing the meaning found in the scripture and helping to bring meaning to others.
5. Trust and vulnerability are needed in small group study; we are vulnerable as we share out of our own experience; in relational Bible study, we learn to trust others and to be trustworthy.

You are invited to this adventure of studying "The Life of David" and seeking new meaning for your own life. As you gather as a Sunday school class, a mid-week Bible study group, in a church building, or in a member's home, may you know God's presence in your midst. May you be led into sharing deeply and caringly with sisters and brothers in faith. May you open yourself to a new hearing of God's word for today. And may God's Spirit move actively among you, even as God moved so powerfully in the life of David.

June Adams Gibble
Elgin, Illinois

1

Samuel

1 Samuel 15:1-28; 16:1-13

Preparation

1. Reflect on the reasons for Saul's loss of kingship.
2. List some of the things Samuel learned about God's way of calling people for ministry.
3. What is your experience in listening to and hearing God's call?
4. How are leaders chosen in our denomination? What lessons from the text might guide us as we call people for ministry in our denomination and in the local church?

Understanding

David's relationship with Samuel is the focus of this first session. 1 Samuel 15:1-28 and 1 Samuel 16:1-13, however, focus on Samuel and the rejection of Saul as king. This movement from the rejection of Saul's reign to David's call to kingship is held together by the person of Samuel. The objective of the story is the call for David to become the king of Israel.

Saul's rejection as king is precipitated by his refusal to destroy all of the Amalekites. God gave the command for their total destruction because of their attack upon Israel (1 Sam. 15:4). In the midst of the battle, Saul decided to spare Agag while destroying everyone else. As Saul's men fought, they noticed that Agag's herds were quite good. The text says, "But Saul and the army spared Agag and the best of the sheep and cattle, the fat calves and lambs—everything that was good. These they were unwilling to destroy completely, but everything that was despised and weak they totally destroyed" (1 Sam. 15:9 NIV).

It is clear that Saul's refusal to carry out the total ban was motivated by greed. It was not just some of the sheep and cattle they kept alive, but the best. The army's unwillingness to destroy everything did not extend to the weak and despised. While our commitment to nonviolence might move us to sympathize with Saul's restraint, we are aware that his refusal to destroy totally was motivated not so much by compassion as it was by greed. While we may have difficulty understanding God's command for total destruction, we recognize that the command comes as a test of Saul's willingness to obey God.

Obedience is relational. It is a trusting response to God's speaking. God desires complete obedience. This understanding of obedience is illustrated in Saul's response to Samuel (1 Sam. 15:15, 20-21). Saul is trying to justify himself. First, he says the best was spared for the purpose of sacrifice. Then he abdicates responsibility by blaming his soldiers. Samuel's response is to reply with words that summarize in a classical way the prophetic criticism of the sacrificial system:

Does the Lord delight in burnt offerings and sacrifices as much as in obeying the voice of the Lord?

To obey is better than sacrifice, and to heed is better than the fat of rams. For rebellion is like the sin of divination, and arrogance like the evil of idolatry. Because you have rejected the word of the Lord, he has rejected you as king (1 Sam. 15:22-23 NIV).

In response to this word of rejection, Saul again tries to clear himself with a weak confession in which he says, "I was afraid of the people and so I gave in to them" (1 Sam. 15:24b NIV). This confession is clearly self-serving. So Samuel reaffirms the Lord's rejection of Saul and turns to walk away. Saul grabs the hem of his robe, tearing it. Samuel interprets this action as a sign that the kingdom of Israel has been torn from Saul and indicates that it has been given " . . . to one better than you" (1 Sam. 15:28 NIV).

This final statement of rejection sets the stage for the call of David to kingship. In the call narrative (1 Sam. 16:1-13), it is so easy to begin comparisons between Saul and David, with David coming out as the saintly one. Yet we must be careful not to idolize David. Throughout this unit we will see weakness, frail arrogance, deception, manipulation, and disobedience in David's relationships with others. How then is he "a better one" than Saul? The answer will be seen in the heart of the man. David shows within all his sinfulness that he has a heart for God, an inner desire to be obedient.

Samuel continues to be the significant character in David's call to kingship. As the story unfolds, Samuel learns several things about the ways of God in calling persons to ministry. Samuel's experience can help us reflect on our experience of calling persons for ministry within the church.

"I have chosen." Samuel's first lesson is that God does the choosing. Even before Samuel goes to Jesse of Bethlehem, God has already chosen David (1 Sam. 16:1). This emphasizes God's sovereignty in calling out persons to be in ministry. The knowledge that God chooses meant that Samuel could go to Bethlehem with open eyes, watching and waiting for God to reveal the one who had been called (1 Sam. 16:1).

"The Lord looks at the heart." Samuel learns that God's standard for leadership is in the inner life of a person and not in their outward appearance. Eliab, Jesse's oldest son, comes forward first. According to traditional expectations, he would be selected as king. Samuel must have been impressed by his stature for he thought Eliab was the man. Then God reminds Samuel:

> Do not consider his appearance or his height, for I have rejected him. The Lord does not look on the things man looks at. Man looks at the outward appearance, but the Lord looks at the heart (1 Sam. 16:7 NIV).

Samuel should have learned this lesson when Saul was rejected. Apparently, outward appearance played a significant role in the selection of Saul (1 Sam. 9:2). Samuel is reminded that the next king will be a person who has a heart for God.

There is still the youngest. Samuel was no doubt wondering what was going on when the Lord did not choose any of Jesse's older sons to be king. His question about more sons has a sense of urgency to it. If not these seven, then who? Jesse responds that there is still the youngest who is tending the sheep. David is not only the youngest but also apparently insignificant so he was left to tend the sheep. Ultimately, the least likely one is chosen as the new king (1 Sam. 16:11).

Often God chooses the least likely ones to do the work. Think of Abraham, Isaac, Jacob, Moses, Ruth, Mary, and others. Paul says, in describing the unity of the body, "on the contrary, those parts of the body that seem to be weaker are indispensable" (1 Cor. 12:22 NIV).

"Rise and anoint him; he is the one." The Lord says to Samuel that David is the one to be anointed. This is the first meeting between Samuel and David. Clearly, their meeting is a matter of God's grace. David is not the one Samuel would have chosen. Yet he is God's revealed choice (1 Sam.16:12).

So it is with our relationships in the covenant community, the church. Most often we do not choose with whom we want to worship and work. Rather, through God's grace we are drawn together with those whom we would not choose.

"The Spirit of the Lord came upon David." The Spirit of the Lord accompanies God's call. A call does not come without the power of the Spirit to carry it out. Saul had also known the power of the Spirit. David, however, was not only empowered by the Spirit; the Spirit would remain with him (1 Sam. 16:13).

David's anointing points to the significance of anointing persons who are called out for ministries in the church—whether lay or professional. Such anointing with oil symbolizes the presence of God's Spirit which both calls and empowers.

Discussion and Action

1. Name some of the "outward appearance" qualifications for ministries in the church (boards, committees, deacons, etc.).
2. Think of some well known leaders in your congregation, or in the national church. How does their physical stature affect your thinking about their leadership? Does being large or small, male or female, make a difference for you in the way you perceive or accept persons in leadership?
3. Discuss what it means to "look at the heart" as God does.
4. How might you raise for discussion the relevant issues about leadership selection in your congregation? Compare the process of calling persons based on their gifts with that of electing persons from a ballot. Develop a plan for sharing your concerns with appropriate persons in the congregation.

2

Saul
1 Samuel 24 and 26

Preparation

1. Read and compare the stories in 1 Samuel 24:1-22 and 26:1-25. What similarities do you find? What are the differences?
2. Examine the dialogue between David and Saul? What did they say to each other? What does this tell you about their relationship?
3. Recall times when you have been in competition with someone. How was the competitiveness acted out?

Understanding

The common image of David's relationship with Saul sees David as the good guy and Saul as the bad guy. This oversimplification causes us to miss the struggle David had in his own heart—the temptation to grasp for himself the kingship which had already been promised. This struggle for integrity in his own life is highlighted in 1 Samuel 24:1-22 and 1 Samuel 26:1-25.

The stage for the struggle between David and Saul is set in the story of David's coming into the court (1 Sam. 16:14-23). The story is prefaced by the anointing of David. Here it is affirmed that " . . . from that day on the Spirit of the Lord came upon David in power" (1 Sam. 16:13 NIV). The court scene that follows is prefaced by the affirmation, "Now the Spirit of the Lord had departed from Saul, and an evil spirit from the Lord tormented him" (1 Sam. 16:14 NIV). Herein lies the seed of conflict between David and Saul. While neither may have been fully aware of the spiritual condition of the other, they soon began to experience a conflictual relationship resulting from the fact that the Spirit was now with David and not Saul.

David is brought into the court to soothe Saul with his music. The description of David in 1 Samuel 16:18 sees him from the outset as a king. All the characteristics mentioned were requirements for a king—bravery, ability to fight, good speech, and a fine-looking countenance. The most important qualification was that God was with him. Saul liked David so much that he made him one of his armor-bearers. This acceptance into the court of Saul set the stage for the future conflict between the two men. Initially, there is no conflict, for David would play his harp and soothe the Saul's troubled spirit whenever Saul felt tormented.

David was anointed to be king. Yet God brought him into the court not as a king but as a servant. It was here in the court of Saul that David would not only learn the responsibilities of kingship but, more importantly, develop the character to be king one day.

No two texts better describe the relationship between David and Saul than the ones in which David spares Saul's life. These stories are filled with jealousy, contempt, hostility, and pursuit.

In the first story (1 Sam. 24:1-22), Saul pursues David with 3,000 soldiers. During the pursuit Saul goes into a cave to relieve himself. It so happens that David and his men were in the same cave. When David's men see Saul, they say, "This is the day the Lord spoke of when he said to you, "'I will give your enemy into your hands for you to deal with as you wish'" (1 Sam. 24:4). The vulnerability of Saul tempted David. There is no hint in the text that David questioned the suggestion of his men. Rather, he immediately began to creep up on Saul. Somewhere, however, David must have reflected on the fact that Saul was still king. Instead of killing him, he humiliates him by cutting off the corner of his robe.

Immediately David's conscience is stricken. He no doubt recognizes how close his hostility for Saul had brought him to killing him. For certain he realized that he had humiliated Saul who is still the king—the Lord's anointed.

When David leaves the cave and shows himself to Saul, he bows down and prostrates himself as a sign of his respect. David confesses to Saul, "Some urged me to kill you but I spared you; I said, I will not lift my hand against my master, because he is the Lord's anointed'" (1 Sam. 24:10b NIV). Later in the speech David promised Saul, " . . .

my hand will not touch you" (1 Sam. 24:12). To symbolize his commitment to Saul, David holds up the corner of his robe to show Saul that he had spared his life.

David has cleared himself with Saul who responds by weeping aloud and saying, "You are more righteous than I—you have treated me well, but I have treated you badly" (1 Sam. 24:17 NIV). Why does Saul respond this way? Is he repentant and grateful to David for his life? For the time being, Saul does seem to be grateful for his life. He also acknowledges the anointing of David to be king when he says, "I know that you will surely be king and that the kingdom of Israel will be established in your hands" (1 Sam. 24:21 NIV). With this acknowledgment, Saul asks David to make an oath that he will not wipe out Saul's descendants and cut off his name. Saul knows the violence he has done to David. So he asks for David's mercy in the future as he has experienced it in the cave.

Saul would have relished the chance to have been in David's position in the cave. There is no doubt that Saul would have killed David. Now Saul finds himself indebted to David for his life. This is not enough, however, for Saul to invite David back into the court. The story concludes with each going their own way—not reconciled, but rather experiencing an uneasy peace.

Once again David spares Saul's life (1 Sam. 26:1-25). This time, it is clear that David's motivation is to show his respect for Saul. True, Saul is still searching for David. The hostility is still present. Yet David's venture into Saul's camp at night with Abishai is an attempt to give Saul a sign that will cut through the hostility. Again David could have used Saul's spear against him. Abishai even suggests that possibility. But this time David clearly asserts, "Don't destroy him! Who can lay a hand on the Lord's anointed and be guiltless?" (1 Sam. 26:9 NIV).

The spear and water jug are a signal to Saul of David's good intentions toward him. David asks Saul, "Why is my Lord pursuing his servant?" (1 Sam. 26:18 NIV). Saul is thankful for his life. He again confesses and invites David to come back, saying, "Because you considered my life precious today, I will not try to harm you again" (1 Sam. 26:24 NIV).

This story raises in dramatic form the question: "How do we relate to our enemies?" David could have taken revenge on Saul, but he does not. Revenge is very common in our world. The prevailing philosophy of the day seems to be "Do the other person in before they do you in." In contrast, David lives out the message of Jesus: " . . . do not resist an evil person" (Matt. 5:39 NIV).

David's respect for Saul was not as strong at the beginning of their relationship as it was at the end. In the midst of the temptation to take things into his own hands, he realized that Saul was the Lord's anointed. This gave him the ability to live in the tension between the promise and fulfillment of his own reign. David would be king. Until that time, he would wait for the Lord to act. Herein lies David's greatness—not that he spared Saul's life, but that in the midst of Saul's disobedience and conniving, David could see and affirm God at work.

Discussion and Action

1. Discuss the reasons for the tension between Saul and David. Examine their dialogue to discern what their motivations might have been.
2. Share stories of times when you, like David and Saul, have experienced competition with someone. Have you ever been taken advantage of when you were weak? Have you ever taken advantage of others in their moment of weakness?
3. Have you experienced a David and Saul conflict in your church? Does "getting the upperhand" ever shape the decision-making process of your congregation? Share stories about your own personal involvement in such situations.
4. Reflect upon times in which you have been able to remain in relationship with persons who have been against you. What convictions, insights, or actions helped you most?
5. How can we affirm someone else's calling and gifts while also affirming our own? Can you identify a time when you felt threatened by someone else's gifts and abilities? What did you do? How did you feel?

3

Jonathan

1 Samuel 18:1-4; 20:1-42

Preparation

1. Read the above texts and list the characteristics of the friendship of David and Jonathan.
2. Write a brief description of friendship based on reflections from the David and Jonathan story.
3. Using a timeline, chart the significant friendships that you have experienced throughout your life. What made or still makes these friendships meaningful? What personality characteristics attracted you to your friends?

Understanding

As a child I vividly remember the expressive reading of the story of David and Jonathan as we sat around the coal stove in the winter time. The story caught my attention. The intrigue of King Saul wanting to kill David, the anger of Saul at his own son Jonathan at the banquet, the arrows flying through the air, the tears of friends as they are forced to part—all dramatically etched the memory of David and Jonathan in my mind forever.

Forty-plus years later these elements of the story are still gripping. However, these fade into the background as the central meaning of the story becomes clear—covenant friendship. Now, as an adult in a world where the experience of friendship is rare, I find that the story of David and Jonathan challenges us to examine the nature of our relationships and gives us insight into the nature of covenant friendship.

The word *friendship* involves images of intimacy and closeness between persons. It would be easy to assume that friendship comes without effort, that it is something we naturally grow into with persons to whom we are attracted consciously or more often unconsciously. Yet we know that it is not easy to make friends even if we are extroverts.

The importance of the word *covenant* in understanding David and Jonathan's relationship is seen in 1 Samuel 18:1-4. The text says that Jonathan "made" a covenant with David. This covenant grew out of a relationship between the two men in which they were beginning to experience a unity of spirit and love for one another. The covenant they made with each other shows that friendship involves a decision.

Jonathan symbolizes his covenant with David by giving him his robe, tunic, sword, bow, and belt. Clothing then, as now, represents the identity of a person. Giving David his clothes symbolizes two realities of covenant: the willingness to give oneself completely to the other person and the recognition of the individuality of the other person. These are the heart of covenant friendship. Jonathan not only had to give himself completely to the relationship; he also had to affirm that David would one day take his place as king. He affirms this by giving David his bow, sword, and belt, all symbols of kingly power.

While the initiative in making covenant with David is taken by Jonathan (1 Sam. 18:1-4), it is clear that their covenant friendship is mutual. David too gives himself fully to Jonathan and recognizes him as a prince who is the natural heir to the throne.

In this story of David and Jonathan, various characteristics help us see more clearly the nature of their relationship (1 Sam. 20:1-42).

Before the Lord. David's speech to Jonathan makes it clear that their covenant was "before the Lord" (1 Sam. 20:8). Their covenant with the Lord is the basis upon which they have been able to come into covenant with each other.

Unfailing kindness. The second characteristic of covenant friendship is unfailing kindness. Jonathan recognizes that such kindness is possible only when it comes from the Lord (1 Sam. 20:14). All covenantal friendships like David and Jonathan's grow as they are inspired by and modeled after the covenant love God has for people.

Covenant is forever. Jonathan's language challenges David to see covenant as continuing into the future (1 Sam. 20:14-15). The phrases "as long as I live" and "do not ever cut off your kindness from my family" call David to remember their covenant forever. Jonathan was concerned not only for himself, but for his children.

my family" call David to remember their covenant forever. Jonathan was concerned not only for himself, but for his children.

A covenant friendship defends and protects. During the second day of the feast, Saul's anger is triggered when he discovers David will not be coming. Knowing of Jonathan's friendship with David, he lashes out at him with a threat on David's life. Jonathan does not back off but comes to David's defense by asking, "Why should he be put to death? What has he done?" (1 Sam. 20:32 NIV). Jonathan risks further abuse, if not death, in order to defend and protect David. He not only quizzes his father; he also makes a public statement about his friendship with David and demonstrates his disapproval of his father's intentions by getting up from the table and leaving (1 Sam. 20:34). Such is the nature of covenant friendship. It lays down its own life for the friend.

Covenant friendship is submissive. Earlier we saw how giving oneself completely to another is at the heart of covenant friendship. We see this in the way David and Jonathan submit to one another. Jonathan's statement of this willingness to submit is classic (1 Sam. 20:4 NIV). He says, "Whatever you want me to do, I'll do for you." He makes this commitment without knowing what David has on his mind. Such trust! But that is the reality of true friendship. Radical self-giving commitment to another rules out self-serving manipulation. So, submission rather than being a threat becomes an opportunity to serve the other person and show the full extent of one's love.

David likewise shows his readiness to submit to Jonathan (1 Sam. 20:41 NIV) when, before parting, he "bowed down before Jonathan three times with his face to the ground." Submission in any covenant friendship is always mutual because both parties are always ready to serve the other.

Covenant friendship grieves. The intimacy of friendship creates deep feelings whenever the relationship is threatened. David and Jonathan grieve for and with each other. Jonathan's grief is described in the words: " . . . on the second day of the month he did not eat, because he was grieved at his father's shameful treatment of David" (1 Sam. 20:34b). Many of the realities of grief—shock, denial, anger—no doubt went through Jonathan as the disclosure of his father's plans sunk in.

David and Jonathan grieve together, symbolized by their tears before parting (1 Sam. 20:41). They would never see each other again. We see David's grief expressed again at Jonathan's death in the lament of the bow (2 Sam. 1:17-27). As the lament ends David says, "I grieve for you, Jonathan my brother; you were very dear to me. Your love for me was wonderful, more wonderful than that of women" (2 Sam. 1:26 NIV).

Grieving is a common experience of deep friendship. The closer we come to a person the more we hurt when they hurt. The more we hurt when anything threatens the relationship.

Covenant friendship endures. Even in the midst of threat and absence true friendship endures. Because the Lord is witness to the covenant, Jonathan tells David to go in peace knowing that the Lord will watch between them. Having lived through the threat of Saul and confident that in this life nothing will be able to separate them, David and Jonathan part.

Discussion and Action

1. Reflect upon the characteristics of David and Jonathan's friendship. As each characteristic of covenant friendship is mentioned, talk about how this particular characteristic has been experienced in your own friendships.
2. Discuss the barriers to covenant friendship. Why are deep friendships so difficult to form today?
3. Discuss covenantal friendship that is evidenced in your own experiences and the experiences of persons you know. How does your group reach out intentionally to others?
4. Intentional covenantal friendships are needed by everyone. Think of the present. Where are such friendships currently forming for you? Think of a way you can reach out to a friend sometime this week.

4

God

2 Samuel 7

Preparation

1. Read 2 Samuel 7 and reflect on the following questions: What is the occasion for God's message to David? What can you learn from the text about the nature of religion in Israel? What is the promise God makes to David?
2. Reflect on a personal experience when an inspired word affirming God's love for you and God's choice of you for some task has come to you through someone else. What was your response?
3. Write down a few words that tell why a church building and sanctuary are important for your expression of faith. How might they also be a hindrance?

Understanding

We have seen the human side of David as he struggled with Saul and developed a lasting friendship with Jonathan. This attracts us to him as a person. Yet it is David's relationship with God which gives him a central place in Israel's history. God's covenant with David as king is seen in today's text (2 Sam. 7).

This covenant is twofold: (1) God reveals himself through a prophetic word to Nathan, and (2) David responds with a prayer. Both revelation and prayer give insight into David's relationship with God.

Finally, David has become king. His major building is completed (2 Sam. 5). He is settled in his place and is at "rest" from all his enemies (2 Sam. 7:1). Since the ark is still residing in a tent outside of Jerusalem, the foremost question to be answered is, "Where will the central shrine be?" Since the comment in the previous chapter is that Michal "had no children to the day of her death" (2 Sam. 6:23 NIV), the second and potentially more troubling question is, "Who will be David's successor?"

In the midst of his newly established security, David reflects one day to the prophet Nathan, "Here I am, living in a palace of cedar, while the ark of God remains in a tent" (2 Sam. 7:2). Nathan knows what is in his mind. David desires to build a temple for the ark. So, without even hesitating, Nathan says, "Go for it." It seems so right for a king to want to build a temple, especially David who has shown deep loyalty to God throughout his life.

It is clear that Nathan's first off-the-cuff response is uninspired, for that night God speaks the word he really wants David to hear. Four main themes emerge in this revelation to David (2 Sam. 7:4-17).

First, God questions David about his desire to build a temple, reminding him that since the exodus, God has moved from place to place. There was never a time when God even desired a house. This questioning of David illustrates the conflict between the God of the tent and the God of the temple, or between the God who is always on the move with his people and the God who permanently resides in one place. There is no question that the God of the tent and the God of the temple are the same God. The question is more one of how the people experience God and how the location of God's presence communicates the nature of God.

Another way of looking at the tension in this story is to see it as a conflict between religion as a movement versus religion as an institution—between faith/revelation and law/tradition. Looking at on specific denomination helps make this point.The ancestors of the Church of the Brethren began meeting in homes in Germany. God clearly resided wherever the community was gathered in the name of Jesus. While the evolution of meetinghouses into larger church-type structures may have been occasioned by practical considerations such as space to accommodate larger crowds, is it not true that a change has occurred in our thinking about where God's presence resides? Too often sacredness has been attached and limited to the buildings in which we worship. Many have lost the biblical vision that believers are the temple of the Holy Spirit (1 Cor. 3:16-17) wherever they come together in the name of Jesus (Matt. 18:20).

A second theme is seen in God's reminder to David that he was taken from the pasture to the throne (2 Sam. 7:8). In this description, David becomes representative of God's covenant with the people of Israel. Central for both David and the people has been God's presence with them wherever they have gone (2 Sam. 7:9). And even without a temple!

A third theme surfaces in 2 Samuel 7:9b-11a, when **God promises to make David's name great and to provide a place for the people of Israel** where they will no longer be disturbed. This promise sets the stage for the climax of the revelation.

The fourth theme that concludes the revelation is the promise that **God will establish a house for David.** Whereas David's desire was to build a house of cedar for God, what David receives is a promise that his house (dynasty) will be established. David will have an offspring to succeed him. Within this promise is a further declaration that this future offspring will be the one to build a temple and that his kingdom will be established forever (2 Sam. 7:15-16). When sin exists, it will be judged. But never will God remove his favor from the family of David.

David's response to this revelation is a prayer (2 Sam. 7:18-29). As is so often true, David received so much more from the Lord than he had anticipated. This prayer response to God's revelation includes the following characteristics which help illustrate David's faith in God.

The prayer begins with humility. David asks, "Who am I, O Sovereign Lord, and what is my family, that you have brought me this far?" (2 Sam. 7:18). Humility is the appropriate response to God's grace.

David's experience of humility becomes gratitude in verse 19 as God's word about the future of David's house sinks in. God's covenant with David is forever. What can be David's response to such a promise if not gratitude.

Another characteristic of David's prayer is remembrance (vv. 23-24). Memory is of central importance. This text illustrates that the promises which God makes with David are based on God's past covenant with his people. So here David remembers the exodus in which "God went out to redeem a people for himself" (2 Sam. 7:23a), the Sinai Covenant in which God "established your people Israel as your very own, forever, and you, O Lord, have become their God" (2 Sam. 7:24 NIV), and finally the conquest of Canaan where God drove out the nations and their gods before the people (2 Sam. 7:23b).

Finally, David concludes his prayer acknowledging God's promise and challenging God to keep his word (2 Sam. 7:29). David recognizes the giftedness of God's covenant. God has initiated the covenant with David and his house not because he is deserving. Rather, the promise to David represents God's choice to remain steadfast and loyal to the people of Israel. David and his family become the instruments through which the people will experience this steadfast love. David knows that the words of promise are trustworthy. He also knows that they can be fulfilled only by the one who has spoken them.

We have all experienced the shattering of a vision. So did Israel at the time of the exile when there was no longer a Davidic king. At such moments, we question the meaning of the promises which seemed to give hope to our vision of the future. So Israel questioned the meaning of the promise of an external covenant with the house of David. Some of these reflections occur in Psalm 89. In this psalm we see that when visions collapse, the promise becomes the foundation for re-envisioning the future. So a day is longed for in which a messiah in the line of David will once again reign. The witness of the Gospels is that this hope is fulfilled in Jesus.

The significance of David as a model of religious experience, therefore, is not that he was a model of moral or ethical behavior. Most significant was David's ability, in faith, to live out of the promise of God when there was seeming to be no human way the promise could be fulfilled.

Discussion and Action

1. Share some discoveries about what your congregation's sanctuary communicates about God.
2. Have two persons role play a discussion between David and Nathan about whether or not to build a temple. The conversation should take place after the revelation to Nathan.
3. Reflect together on this question following the role play: How does the place in which we worship affect our experience of God?
4. How does your awareness of God's promise help you live toward the future with hope? What specific promises of God have been and/or are meaningful in your own life?
5. How are our responses alike or different from David's responses?

5

Mephibosheth
2 Samuel 9

Preparation

1. Read the scripture and reflect on the following questions: What are David's motivations in searching for Saul's relatives? What role does David's covenant with Jonathan play in this story? How does David respond and relate to Mephibosheth?
2. Reflect on your responses to persons who are dispossessed, powerless, or handicapped.
3. What special problems would need to be overcome for powerless, dispossessed, or handicapped persons to be fully included in the fellowship of your congregation?

Understanding

The story of David's relationship to Mephibosheth, the crippled son of Jonathan, illustrates David's covenant loyalty to Jonathan. This raises questions for today about how we treat those who are powerless due to an emotional, mental, or physical handicap, or due to societal issues.

It is clear from David's initial question that his search for descendants of Saul's house is primarily motivated by remembering his promise to Jonathan to never cut off his kindness to his family (1 Sam. 20:15). Yet David's question might sound a little like Herod's declaration to go worship the new born babe. This has caused some to question David's motivation. Why did he really want to know whether any of Saul's descendants remained? Might David have been concerned about eliminating any possible threat to his reign?

When David finally learns of Mephibosheth, he orders that Mephibosheth be brought to the court. Is this to care for him or to be able to control any influence he might have over those who were still loyal to Saul? From the story, there is no reason to believe that Mephibosheth's needs were not already being cared for. Even though David's primary motivation grew out of his covenant with Jonathan, we see the possibility of ulterior motives, namely, to keep an eye on Mephibosheth. This may be why Ziba, Saul's servant, tells David before revealing his name that Jonathan's son is crippled in both feet (2 Sam. 9:3b). Ziba wants David to know that Mephibosheth is not a threat to him.

Yet Mephibosheth feels threatened when he comes into David's presence. He bows before David paying him honor as king. David eases his apprehension saying, "Do not be afraid" (2 Sam. 2:7). This is the first contact Mephibosheth has had with David since he became king. He knows that the usual practice for a new king is to put to death the family of the former king in order to erase all threat. So David's words to Mephibosheth are a sign of God's grace. David will show Mephibosheth God's kindness by remaining loyal to the covenant he made with his father Jonathan. Apart from David's remembrance of this covenant, Mephibosheth's life might have been threatened.

In 2 Samuel 9:7 David makes a threefold promise to Mephibosheth. First, David states his promise to show loving kindness to Mephibosheth for the sake of his father Jonathan. The repetition of this promise is important. It shows that what David is about to do comes from loyalty to Jonathan. The word *kindness* used here and earlier (vv. 1, 3) describes a commitment to be loyal to one's promises regardless of the circumstances. Even though Jonathan is no longer alive, Mephibosheth has no need to fear because the covenant made with his father lives on in David's heart.

Second, David promises Mephibosheth all the land that belonged to his grandfather Saul (2 Sam. 9:7b). Saul's estate had been managed up to this time by Ziba, Saul's servant (2 Sam. 9:2—16:1). Ziba was not only taking care of Mephibosheth, but he also was looking out for his own interests. So David makes it clear to Ziba (2 Sam. 9:9-10) that the estate is Mephibosheth's and that he is to be his servant and caretaker. By making this move, David guarantees Mephibosheth that he will be cared for even beyond his lifetime.

The third promise David makes is that Mephibosheth will always eat at his table (2 Sam. 9:7c). The restatement of this promise two more times (2 Sam. 9:10, 13) shows its importance. What does eating at the king's table mean? As indicated earlier, Mephibosheth was receiving care and concern from David; he was not hungry. So eating at the king's table means more than being fed.

Two things are symbolized by eating at the king's table. First, it is a sign of Mephibosheth's full restoration and, as such, is a sign of honor. Outwardly, it shows David's intention of honoring his covenant with Jonathan. Most certainly, David remembers when Saul's invitation to come and eat was a trap to kill him. Here David's table is a sign that he has forgiven Saul and the past.

Secondly, eating at someone's table symbolizes fellowship. There are no hints in the story that David ever thought of having a friendship with Mephibosheth as he had with Jonathan. Also, there is no reason to believe that he would actually be eating his meals with Mephibosheth. However, the imagery of eating at table would lead us to believe that David did become personally involved in Mephibosheth's life and that there may have been a compassionate relationship that developed out of his love for Jonathan.

By finding Mephibosheth, David does secure his reign from any threat by Saul's people. He creates security by fulfilling his covenant promises rather than through political control or violence. In doing so, his relationship with Mephibosheth becomes a sign of God's covenant love to those who are on the outside.

We are reminded by the story of David and Mephibosheth that God's covenant with his people is the foundation of all human covenants. This story helps us to remember that God's covenant is universal. How ready and willing are we to commit ourselves to the powerless, dispossessed, and handicapped? God's new covenant with us in Jesus Christ calls us to extend covenant love to others as we have experienced that same love in Jesus Christ.

The story of David and Mephibosheth highlights some characteristics found in experiences of powerlessness. One of the characteristics is fear. Frequently, powerless persons live in fear of those around them. All too often the "Zibas" responsible for their care take advantage of them and misuse them to fulfill their own needs. Often when any kindness or covenant loyalty is missing in the disadvantaged person's life the fear increases. How do we relate to powerless persons? Do we reach out to them? Or do we act as if they don't exist?

Often, powerless people are mistreated and used by others. Ziba took over Saul's estate and managed it for his own advantage. David stepped in and restored it to Mephibosheth. Sometimes the powerless ones actually lose what is rightfully theirs because people think they cannot care for themselves. Often others are surprised that powerless persons can become powerful, creative persons.

On the hopeful side, some powerless and dispossessed persons today are experiencing acceptance and respect. Educational opportunities are increasing, jobs are opening up, and access to public buildings is becoming more common. Ministries with the blind and deaf are more common. This is a sign that many persons in the church are beginning to extend covenant love to the powerless ones and are saying by their actions, "There is a place for you in the fellowship of the church, there is a place for you to eat with us."

Discussion and Action

1. Begin with a dramatic reading of the text. Assign four parts: narrator, David, Ziba, Mephibosheth. Glance over the text to identify and practice your parts. Then read the text for the group.
2. Reflect on the story using the questions in Preparation 1.
3. Discuss ways in which God's new covenant in Jesus Christ calls us to relate to the powerless and dispossessed.
4. Discuss whether or not powerless persons have access to the fellowship and ministries (worship, education, etc.) of your congregation. In what way is your congregation meeting the needs of those who are powerless?
5. A possibility for ministry would be to visit a powerless person in your local community. Get to know that person—their spiritual, physical, and relational needs. Are there ways you can meet any of these needs? This might be either an individual or a group effort.

6

Bathsheba and Uriah

2 Samuel 11:1-27

Preparation

1. Read 2 Samuel 11:1-27 in several biblical translations. Reflect on what is happening in the story.
2. Reflect on how you feel toward David. Where do you get angry at him? Where do you feel compassion? Where do you identify with his feelings or actions?
3. Imagine yourself as Bathsheba. What are your feelings at the different stages in this story? Then do the same from Uriah's perspective.

Understanding

The story of David's adultery with Bathsheba captures the imagination of adults every bit as firmly as the story of his killing Goliath captures the imagination of children. Its power as a story comes from the way it includes elements of human experience with which we are all familiar: sexual misconduct, the abuse of power, deception and cover-up, the loss of control over one's destiny, and homicide.

In this story, David becomes an enigma as the nature of his heart is exposed. We know he is God's chosen king. His house will remain forever on the throne. We have seen David's patience in not taking Saul's life to gain the throne. He was loyal to Mephibosheth because of his covenant with Jonathan. And then all of a sudden we see in this story a David who not only commits adultery with Bathsheba, but commits murder when his efforts at covering up fail. Until now David has been portrayed, for the most part, as one who keeps covenants. However, now he is seen clearly as one who violates covenants.

Herein lies the power of the story of David and Bathsheba. It helps us identify within ourselves the seductive entanglement of sin that so often threatens to undo us just when everything seems to be going well. Let us take a closer look at the various movements in this story. As we do so, we will be challenged to go beyond the adultery to see the larger story—the misuse of power.

The setting for this story is puzzling. The opening verses read, "In the spring, at the time when kings go off to war, David sent Joab out with the king's men and the whole Israelite army . . . . But David remained in Jerusalem" (2 Sam. 11:1 NIV). The tension heightens and curiosity rises in the story with David's decision to stay away from the fighting. After all, David is king and it is his responsibility to fight. One can hardly imagine that earlier in his career David would have missed an opportunity to engage in battle. What is happening in David's life? Why does he change his behavior? What has caused him to withdraw from front-line action? Was David so accustomed to power that he thought he could do whatever pleased himself? On the other hand, perhaps, David was beginning to tire of all the responsibility and wanted to try a different way of being. In some ways, David responded much like we might when we become weary of the heavy responsibility we carry for others.

The adulterous act begins as David walks around on the roof one evening and sees Bathsheba bathing. Her beauty attracts him. Temptation to adultery begins with the eyes. This kind of temptation is part of human nature and God alerted humanity to that with the story of the Garden, "when the woman saw that the fruit of the tree was good for food and pleasing to the eyes (Gen. 3:6 NIV).

The story moves very quickly. Nothing in the text suggests that David planned the adulterous act in advance. Rather, with the attraction of physical beauty in full view, he immediately sends for information concerning the identity of the woman. Having found out that she is the wife of Uriah the Hittite, he sends some messengers to get her.

The key word in this part of the story is *sent* (Brueggemann, *David's Truth*, pp. 56-68). Twice David sends. Sending is what kings and others in authority do. To be able to send someone grows out of the power a person possesses. Here sending not only signifies David's power, but it also shows clearly that he is the one taking the initiative.

At this point in the story, David is fully in control of the action or, at least, he thinks he is.

Bathsheba is brought to David. They become intimate with one another and the enjoyment of the moment seems to be complete (2 Sam. 11:4). Supposedly, no one knows except a few servants Bathsheba returns home. Then David's world comes crashing down upon him when he hears the word sent from Bathsheba, "I am pregnant" (2 Sam. 11:5 NIV). With these words David knows that he has broken covenant in a way that others will be able to see. Quickly, David, using his power as a king, decides to arrange for a cover-up.

David's quick move to cover up his adultery shows that his conscience is stricken. He knows he has broken covenant (Exod. 20:14). Uriah is called from battle under the pretense of getting a report about the fighting. David encourages Uriah to go home and relax and even gets him drunk. Uriah refuses to go home and sleeps with the servants at the entrance to the palace. In a significant encounter between David and Uriah, Uriah says, "The ark and Israel and Judah are staying in tents, and my master Joab and my lord's men are camped in the open fields. How could I go to my house to eat and drink and lie with my wife? As surely as you live, I will not do such a thing!" (2 Sam. 11:11 NIV). Uriah is clear about David's intentions and refuses to be disloyal to his commander and fellow soldiers.

This text contrasts Uriah's covenant loyalty as a Hittite with David's covenant-breaking. This is stated in a final way in the closing words of this section, " . . . he did not go home" (2 Sam. 11:13). In contrast, David's effort to get Uriah drunk shows how much David had lost control.

The murder of Uriah involves all the intrigue and violence of a political assassination. David's attempt at cover-up has failed. The only obvious solution is to murder Uriah. In David's mind this will free him to take Bathsheba as his wife. As Uriah sleeps David pens a letter to Joab over whom he still has control. Ironically, the letter ordering Uriah's death is carried by Uriah to Joab the next day. Uriah is unsuspecting and to the end is innocent of what is happening.

David's plans go well. Joab puts the men too close to the wall of the city at a place where the fighting is heaviest. Several men are killed including Uriah. When the incident is reported to him, David says, "Don't let this upset you; the sword devours one as well as another" (2 Sam. 11:25). This "war is war" and "don't worry" type of response shows the hypocrisy in David's heart. Inwardly, he is delighted with

Uriah's death, yet he responds in a "so what" manner to hide his real feelings.

After a period of mourning, David takes Bathsheba as his wife and a son is born. David must have felt secure in the illusion that everything was all right. However, a final verdict is rendered by the narrator in closing this episode. The verdict is that "the thing which David has done displeased the Lord" (2 Sam. 11:27). This valuation of what has happened contradicts David's when he told Joab not to be upset (v. 25).

The words of the prophet Isaiah illustrate the human tendency to see things differently than God: "Woe to those who call evil good and good evil, who put darkness for light and light for darkness, who put bitter for sweet and sweet for bitter" (Isa. 5:20 NIV). David as covenant-breaker has claimed that it really doesn't matter. God, the covenant-maker, says that it does.

As the story ends with God's verdict, we have the sense that it is not over. David soon learns this when Nathan appears.

Discussion and Action

1. Identify with David, Bathsheba, and Uriah. What feelings surface in you as you identify with these three characters.
2. Discuss how the David and Bathsheba story relates to life in our day. Where do you see similar misuse of power?
3. Discuss what the story tells us about adultery. What happens to those involved? What are some of its consequences? How can such relationships be reconciled? In what ways can the church serve as a place of healing and reconciliation in this kind of situation rather than a place of alienation and judgment?
4. Isaiah pronounces woe on those who call evil good and good evil (5:20). What are some areas in today's world where evil is being pronounced good and good evil? How does this lead to confusion in moral and ethical behavior? What role has the church played in contributing to this confusion? What role can the church play in helping to bring clearer direction to moral and ethical issues?

7

Nathan
2 Samuel 12:1-14

Preparation

1. Read 2 Samuel 12:1-14 twice. First, imagine that you are Nathan. Then read it as if you were David. Reflect on the differences in how you hear the story. With which person do you personally feel more comfortable?
2. Identify a sin which you feel needs to be confronted. Write a parable detailing a confrontation similar to the one Nathan had with David.

Understanding

The story of David's adultery with Bathsheba and the consequent murder of Uriah closes with David being satisfied that the cover-up has been complete. David is now back in control of his life—or is he? As readers, we know differently. The comment of the writer at the end of the story declares God's displeasure with David (2 Sam. 11:27). So we are not surprised that God sends Nathan to David.

However, we must participate in this story as more than readers. The story of David's adultery, murder, and cover-up is, after all, the story of our own sin and cover-up. When we reflect upon our own story, we can understand David's surprise in the encounter with Nathan. Cover-up creates a blindness and smugness which makes us feel we are getting away with something.

Nathan begins the indictment of David with a parable. The parable as such does not name a specific sin. It rather paints the picture of a gross injustice which has been done to a poor man. Nathan could have come like John the Baptist naming David's sin and calling him to repentance. Instead, the parable he tells sets David up by drawing him into it personally. The parable focuses on what could have been a real story. Nathan had no doubt brought many such stories to David. The parable's effectiveness is that it draws David into it without him realizing that it is about him.

How much we in the church need to learn the act of storytelling through parables as a way of confronting each other! How often has unnecessary conflict broken out in the church as a result of accusers blatantly confronting wrongdoers. Storytelling through parables draws both the teller and hearer into itself and might be a way in which we can first take the plank out of our own eye so we can see clearly to help take the speck from a brother's or sister's eye.

David's response to this story is highly emotional (2 Sam. 12:5—6). He "burned with anger." The intensity of this response is a sign of what is going on inside him. There is no indication of how soon after his adultery that Nathan comes to him. No doubt David's guilt still plagues him. On hearing this parable, David's residue of guilt is touched; he is reminded of what he has tried to cover up and forget. Burning anger results as a means of diffusing his own inner conflict and calling attention away from it. All this occurs in David at an unconscious level as it does also in us. So David declares that the rich man deserves to die—the penalty which would be ordered for David and Bathsheba except for the careful cover-up.

David's response in burning anger is his first reaction to the injustice of the parable. However, in this spontaneous response, David has not only revealed the way guilt is tearing him apart; but he has also indicted himself.

Immediately upon hearing David's response, Nathan says, "You are the man." Again, notice at the beginning of the indictment that David's specific sins are not named (2 Sam. 12:7a). The indictment "You are the man" communicates to David that he is the one who deserves to die. This indictment also calls David to accept responsibility for his actions. From the time he heard Bathsheba say "I am pregnant," David tried to pin it on Uriah her husband. The cover-up is over. No longer can David hide. The illusion of control over his life and its consequent security is shattered. Deep down David knows that he is the man who deserves to die. He is about to experience the reality of Paul's affirmation: "For the wages of sin is death but the gift of God is eternal life in Christ Jesus our Lord" (Rom. 6:23 NIV).

In this indictment speech, the specific nature of David's sin becomes clear. First, however, it is noteworthy that the indictment continues by rehearsing the ways God has been gracious to David. He is called to remember God and the heights from which he has fallen. David is reminded that God anointed him, delivered him from Saul, and gave Saul's house to him. David is reminded that God would have done even more for him.

When the heart of the indictment comes (v. 9), the primary sin is that David has despised the word of the Lord by doing evil in his eyes. David had set himself up as his own authority—a common temptation for those in power. When tempted with lust and violence, he set himself above the law. It was out of a despising heart that the acts of adultery and murder were committed. We are reminded here of Jesus teaching that the heart of a person is the source of all that is evil (Matt. 15:19).

The verdict which comes as part of the indictment is twofold. First, the sword will never depart from David's house. The given reason is "because you despised me and took the wife of Uriah the Hittite to be your own" (v. 10 NIV). The sin of murder seems to gain ascendancy over David's adultery here because of the way he used it to cover up. The verdict of violence echoes Jesus' address to the disciples: "Put your sword back in its place, for all who draw the sword will die by the sword" (Matt. 26:52 NIV). David learns that violence begets violence. Once a violent act is unleashed it has social consequences that cannot be stopped.

The second verdict is that David's wives will be taken from him by one who is close to him. Again David learns the social consequences of uncontrolled lust. David committed adultery in secret, but he will experience the public consequences of his act. As such, it will be a sign for all to see that God does punish sin.

David's confession is simple, "I have sinned against the Lord" (NIV). This was no doubt a painful moment for David. Notice the nature of the confession. It does not focus on the adultery or the murder. Rather, it deals with the underlying attitude which David had developed toward God. Again, he is aware in a new way that life cannot be lived on one's own terms. God is the one who has defined the positive limits for living within his covenant (Exod. 20). So David rightly recognizes his primary sin to be against God. He gives expression to this in Psalms 32 and 51.

Following David's confession, Nathan pronounces a twofold verdict. First, David is forgiven and he and Bathsheba will not die. Secondly, the son born to them will die.

Discussion and Action

1. Share personal responses after reading the story from the perspective of Nathan and David. With whom do you identify? With David, as one who needs to be confronted with sin? Or with Nathan, as one who feels called to confront sin in others?
2. Share a David experience in which a Nathan came to you and confronted you with a sin that you were trying to cover up. Who was your Nathan? How did you respond?
3. Share a Nathan experience in which you felt called to confront someone with their sin. What was your approach? How did it compare with Nathan's approach? What were the results?
4. Share the parables of confrontation which you have written as suggested in Preparation 2.
5. Think globally. Who are some Nathans confronting our world today? What sins are they addressing? Does there seem to be a responsiveness?

8

David And the Infant Son of Bathsheba

2 Samuel 12:15-25

Preparation

1. Read 2 Samuel 12:15-25 and reflect on what David learned from his adultery with Bathsheba and the consequences.
2. Watch the TV and newspapers for stories about the death of children. What are the causes of death? How do family members seem to cope with the loss?
3. Reflect on situations in your own life when you grieved or pleaded with God because of the way in which your behavior caused serious consequences for someone else.

Understanding

The story of the death of David and Bathsheba's infant son is difficult. For all of us, the death of babies raises strong feelings as well as troublesome questions. Why does David seem to grieve before the child's death? Why does it seem so easy to let go once the infant dies? Why are David and Bathsheba blessed with another child—Solomon? These questions are easier to raise than to answer. Let us go to the story and see what we might learn.

When David and Bathsheba's infant son becomes ill, David, struggling with God in prayer, pleads with God to save the child (2 Sam. 12:15-17). The intensity of his prayer is evidenced by fasting, withdrawing from others, and humbling himself before God by spending the nights on the ground.

Also, there may be an element of anticipatory grieving in David's actions. For he had heard the word from God through Nathan before the child was born that the child would die. Knowing God as a keeper of his word, the certainty of the child's death is before him. So intense is David's praying and grieving that not even the elders of his household can dissuade him. Hopefully, David intercedes for the child.

For all of us, a terminal illness or the death of a child causes us to doubt or question our faith. It is a natural response to wonder and to question the death of our precious little ones.

Those who have had critically ill infants know the agony of intercession. Whether or not the infant's illness is caused by the sin of the parent, the sinfulness of each person raises within them the thought that "somehow I am responsible and God is punishing me." When this struggle takes place, there is need to sort out real guilt from imagined guilt—guilt that in no way relates to the illness for which we are praying. When imagined guilt is put aside, then we are more likely to experience God's presence.

Ezekiel 18 and John 9 can help us to understand that the behavior or actions of parents do not result in the death of a child. Each person has an individual relationship with God, and it is that relationship that God considers and nurtures.

Ezekiel corrects the thinking of the Israelites in the following statement:

> The word of the Lord came to me again: "What do you mean by repeating this proverb concerning the land of Israel, 'The fathers have eaten sour grapes, and the children's teeth are set on edge?' As I live says the Lord God, this proverb shall no more be used by you in Israel. Behold, all souls are mine; the soul of the father as well as the soul of the son is mine: the soul that sins shall die" (Ezek. 18:2-4).

This prophetic word corrects the misunderstanding that a child's death is caused by the irresponsible acts of a parent(s). John 9:3 moves in a similar direction by reminding us that neither the blind man nor his parents had anything to do with his blindness or the receiving of sight. What is important is that the works of God were made manifest in the recovery of sight.

The experience of death is not easy. On stress test scales, it ranks at the top. Everyone reacts differently and sometimes in unpredictable ways. Such is the case with David. The servants, knowing the intensity of David's reactions during the infant's illness, feared that he would become desperate on hearing the news.

Their fear led them to whisper among themselves so David wouldn't hear. Yet, when David heard the whispering, even though he couldn't hear the actual content, he knew the child was dead. When David asked about the child, the servants quickly confirmed that the child had died (2 Sam. 12:18-19).

Whispering as a style of hiding communication actually was the communication. Think of the hospital setting. How often have I seen family members and friends whispering in the near presence of a patient after hearing the diagnosis of cancer or some other terminal disease. The attempt to hide reality by whispering inadvertently communicates it. So David knew his son had died even before it was confirmed by the servants.

Upon hearing of his son's death, David surprised everyone. At the moment when the grief process would normally begin, David's grief seemingly came to an end. He got up from the ground, washed, put on lotions, changed his clothes, worshiped, and asked for food (2 Sam. 12:20-23).

Shocked by this strange behavior, the servants inquire of David, "Why are you acting this way?" David's response is twofold. First, he explains that the intensity of his pleading was motivated by the hope that God would be gracious and spare his son. Secondly, now that the child has died there is nothing else to do.

David's view of death surfaces in the comment, "Can I bring him back again? I will go to him, but he will not return to me" (2 Sam. 12:23 NIV). He affirms the finality of death and moves on to accept it.

The child's death confirms for David that God is now done dealing with him. The judgment has ended. Everything is now made right between David and God. The child born of Bathsheba symbolized David's attempt to live and control his life apart from God's covenant. During the child's illness David learns he cannot control life. This is symbolized by his sleeping on the ground. With the child's death, he is again free to live, knowing both the forgiveness of God and the judgment which comes to those who presume to live by and for themselves.

Soon after the death of their child, David and Bathsheba have another son (2 Sam. 12:24-25). They name him Solomon. This name is related to peace, well-being, and prosperity. Therefore, we see in Solomon's birth a sign of God's favor upon David and Bathsheba. This may come as a surprise. Yet, Solomon's birth is a sign that God's forgiveness is real and the past is over.

The reality of God's forgiveness is made real beyond doubt in the affirmation that the Lord loved Solomon. Because of this love, God gave Solomon the name Jedidiah which means "loved by the Lord" (v. 25). The significance of God's love is underscored by the fact that God sent the word through the prophet Nathan to name him Jedidiah. Nathan was the one who had said to David, "You are the man" (2 Sam. 12:7) and later " . . . the son born to you will die" (2 Sam. 12:14). Now Nathan, the prophet, speaks the name Jedidiah, "loved by the Lord," and confirms for David that God is renewing covenant with him.

Discussion and Action

1. Read 2 Samuel 12:15-25 as a dramatic story. There are three parts—narrator, David, and David's servants. Assign someone each part. Suggest that each part be read with feeling for the person involved in the story.
2. In 2 Samuel 12:15-17 is David praying, or is he grieving, or both? Have you ever been so overwhelmed with loss and anguish for someone that you fasted while you prayed? When have you prayed for someone so deeply that you could not eat or sleep?
3. Share your experience of praying for someone who was or is terminally ill. How do you pray? What are your feelings as you pray? What keeps you praying when nothing seems to be happening?
4. Share experiences when, in spite of your prayers, death has come or situations have gone unchanged or gotten worse. What have been your thoughts, feelings, actions at such times?
5. David stopped praying and fasting when the child died. How was his experience different than yours has been?

9

Losing Control
2 Samuel 13—19:15

Preparation

1. Read 2 Samuel 13. Reflect on the personal relationship described in this story. In what way does this story touch your life? Spend some time thinking about the difference between love and lust.
2. Read 2 Samuel 15. Why does Absalom carry out a conspiracy against David? Why does it fail? What is David's response to the conspiracy?
3. Review the relationships in your family. Name some of the destructive forces at work. How have you experienced God's grace and reconciliation in your family?

Understanding

The sequence of stories in 2 Samuel 13—19:15 center around David's relationship with Absalom. This story that begins with an act of violence from Amnon toward Tamar follows the episode of Nathan's confrontation with David concerning David's adulterous relationship with Bathsheba (2 Sam. 11—12). This signals us that we will continue to see ways in which David's behavior affects the relationships of the whole family. Through acts of violence such as rape, competition for power, lack of control, hatred, and murder, David's family carries scars of destruction and shame.

The story of Amnon and Tamar is a classic story of rape (2 Sam. 13:1-14). Before looking at the story itself, however, we must see it in context. First, it illustrates the truth spoken by Nathan to David (2 Sam. 12:11-12). Secondly, we must see the story in the light of the struggle for power between David's first-born son, Amnon, and third-born son, Absalom. We will see how the power struggle becomes prevalent in the story of Absalom.

The story of Amnon and Tamar is an illustration of an act of violence that destroys human dignity, depriving a woman of her wholeness and sense of well-being. The text says that Amnon "fell in love" with Tamar. The story of Amnon and Tamar is descriptive of a relationship in which romantic feelings focus on the act of sexuality. Amnon dramatically reveals his intention by saying that he is "frustrated to the point of illness on account of his sister Tamar, for she was a virgin, and it seemed impossible for him to do anything to her" (2 Sam. 13:2 NIV). Amnon's lust was so deep it created an inner conflict that made him sick. This is far different than the "love-sick" we use to describe couples who are head over heels in love with each other. Amnon's intent seems to be full of danger and destruction having little to do with cultivating a sensitive, tender, loving relationship.

Amnon begins to develop a scheme. Jonadab, a family member, helps with the arrangements and prepares for the action to occur. Amnon, the manipulator, and Jonadab, the accomplice, draw Tamar into the action.

The plot thickens with the use of force. The story makes no pretense that Amnon simply tried to seduce Tamar. In the story we read that, when she brought the food to him as was part of the plan, he grabbed her and said, "Come to bed with me, my sister" (2 Sam. 13:11 NIV). Tamar resisted Amnon. She says "don't" three times (v. 12). Then she argues trying to get Amnon to consider the consequences for him and for her. As a last resort she suggests the possibility that the king would allow them to be married.

Amnon refuses to listen and to accept her suggestion. "But he refused to listen to her, and since he was stronger than she, he raped her" (2 Sam. 13:14). This is an act of violence and nothing more.

The violence of rape is tragically illustrated in these verses. Amnon's hatred of Tamar now that he has had his way with her is even greater than his love for her (2 Sam. 13:15-19). This should not be a surprise since his love was a passion filled with lust and motivated by self-gratification.

Now Amnon cannot stand the sight of Tamar so he orders her to "get up and get out" (2 Sam. 13:15 NIV). Again Tamar tries to reason with Amnon and he refuses to listen. Amnon's refusal to listen to her shows how self-gratification destroys reason. Paul affirms this reality,

"The mind of sinful man is death, but the mind controlled by the spirit is life and peace; the sinful mind is hostile to God" (Rom. 8:6 NIV). So Amnon has his personal servant put Tamar out and bolt the door.

Tamar goes into mourning. She puts ashes on her head, tears her robe, and weeps loudly. Her brother Absalom, upon seeing her, concludes what has happened; he asks Tamar, "Has that Amnon, your brother, been with you?" (2 Sam. 13:20 NIV). Absalom's response is not all that comforting. He says, "Don't take this thing to heart" (2 Sam. 13:20 NIV). It is a callous and insensitive response. Tamar suffers as do all victims of violence from the psychological abuse of not being taken seriously. Absalom's response can almost be taken to imply Tamar's complicity in the act.

Yet Absalom is clearly angered and hates Amnon to the point that he says nothing to Amnon about it—either good or bad. Acting as though nothing has happened, Absalom in reality is waiting for the day to carry out his vengeance. Finally, the working out of Absalom's hatred takes place two years later as Absalom plots to kill Amnon and succeeds.

David is passive throughout the whole episode. Even when he hears of Tamar's rape he does nothing. Yes, he does get furious, but there is no hint of any effort on his part to discipline Amnon or bring about reconciliation in the family. David's failure to discipline Amnon is a weakness which sets in motion a host of destructive dynamics in his family.

After killing Amnon, Absalom, fearing reprisal, flees to Geshur. After three years, David brings Absalom back to Jerusalem and restores him as a member of the royal family (2 Sam. 14). David's failure to administer discipline in his own family carried over into a failure to execute justice in the land. Absalom took advantage of the situation to begin to gain support for himself. He stood along the road leading to the city gate where justice was normally administered. He spoke especially to those tribes of Israel who were not being heard. Absalom stole the hearts of the people, particularly the men of Israel. The conspiracy grew to the point that David fled from the city.

This conspiracy against David shows how he not only lost control of his family, but also he was losing control of his throne. Yet, in fleeing, David shows his continued reliance on God. He tells Zadok, "Take the Ark of God back into the city. If I find favor in the Lord's eyes, he will bring me back and let me see it and his dwelling place again. But if he says, 'I am not pleased with you,' then I am ready; let him do to me whatever seems good to him" (2 Sam. 15:25-26 NIV). David never loses an awareness that God is the one who has given him the throne. His rule can last only as long as he continues to find favor with God.

The conspiracy of Absalom comes to a tragic end for David when Absalom is killed in a battle with his troops. David is grief-stricken as he cries out, "Oh my son Absalom! My son, my son Absalom! If only I had died instead of you—O Absalom, my son, my son!" (2 Sam. 18:33 NIV). We can feel David's agony. Yet how could he grieve so when Absalom had conspired against Amnon, his son, and killed him. David not only grieves but wishes he could have taken his place.

We see in this story David's love for his family. In spite of his own sinfulness and the sinfulness of his children, David still loved them. How often we see parents who grieve deeply for rebellious, wayward children. Sometimes, parents grieve for a lifetime because no reconciliation occurs or physical death prevents reconciliation. Frequently in biblical stories, God is seen as weeping in anguish for the "wayward ones." David's grieving love and his desire to take Absalom's place prefigures the love of one from the lineage of David who would one day take his place in death on the cross, dying for the sin of the whole world—Jesus Christ the Lord.

Discussion and Action

1. What are appropriate ways to deal with persons who are emotionally, mentally, physically, and spiritually harmed through acts of violence? How can these persons be restored to wholeness?
2. Share some of your own family dynamics, both some of the negative or destructive forces and some of the grace-filled times.
3. From the beginning of time, conspiracy has been a common experience in political life. Is there a message from the story of Absalom's conspiracy that we need to hear today?
4. In what ways do we cultivate an environment or atmosphere that allows conspiracies to develop?
5. Discuss the pain and anguish parents carry concerning their children who choose to live their lives in ways that appear destructive.

10

David and Solomon
1 Kings 1—2:12

Preparation

1. Read 1 Kings 1—2:12 several times. Who is involved? Where do you find yourself becoming involved with your own feelings? Why?
2. Reflect on your personal experience when you and/or others tried to put yourselves in charge and take over.
3. Write down what you have learned from this study of David. Take this to your closing group session.

Understanding

Solomon's rise to power takes place in the midst of the political intrigue precipitated by David's impotency and powerlessness. David is old and well advanced in years (1 Kgs. 1 NIV). His servants bring Abishag, a Shunammite, into the court to wait on him and to keep him warm. This strategy was designed to alleviate the fears of any who felt David could not rule because he was no longer sexually potent. However, the comment of the text that David had no intimate relations with Abishag (1 Kgs. 1:4) shows the plan failed. David is old. He is impotent and with one exception throughout this story (1 Kgs 1:28) he remains passive. David, now as an old man, has become weak and powerless.

The development of powerlessness in the life of a political leader or the government creates an opportunity for power to emerge pretenders who rise to the occasion. So it is with Adonijah. Sensing the powerlessness of David in his old age, he puts himself forward (1 Kgs. 1:5-10).

Adonijah makes his move with the declaration, "I will be king." And one who is going to be king must look and act like a king. So Adonijah gets fifty bodyguards to go ahead of him. In addition he confers with and gains the support of Joab, David's military commander, and Abiathar, a priest, both of whom had supported David. To solidify his support and to inspire his move to power, he invites his supporters and all the king's sons and royal officials of Judah to come to a great campaign feast. In any case, the absence of Nathan and Solomon from the guest list is a subtle indication that Adonijah's campaign is doomed from the beginning. His move is a classic model of power politics in which the strong upstage and uproot the weak.

Nathan appears again but in quite a different role. Earlier, as prophet, he confronted David with the need to repent. Now as prophet-friend, he appears as a power broker intervening to secure David's throne by having Solomon anointed as king (1 Kgs. 1:11-27).

Nathan knows how to pull the right ropes. He goes to Bathsheba and informs her that Adonijah has already become king. This slant in the story is clearly more than the text says. He urges her to go to David with the news. While Bathsheba is telling David what is happening, Nathan conveniently appears. He asks David directly, "Have you, my lord the king, declared that Adonijah shall be king after you, and that he will sit on your throne?" (1 Kgs. 1:24 NIV). Nathan implies that David has acted secretly. David's respect for Nathan is so great that this insinuation goes straight to the heart. David has not blessed Adonijah's move in any way. So far David has done nothing throughout this entire story. At the very beginning, the text emphasizes David's passivity saying, "His father had never interfered with him by asking, 'Why do you behave as you do?' " (1 Kgs. 1:6). This lack of parental accountability is what has made it possible for Adonijah's movement to become so strong.

Nathan's encounter energizes David. Immediately David takes control of the situation and takes several steps to make Solomon king.

First, he takes an oath in Nathan's and Bathsheba's presence assuring them that he will move to make Solomon king.

Secondly, he instructs Zadok the priest, Nathan the prophet, and Benaiah, son of Jehoiada, to take Solomon to Gihon and anoint him king (1 Kgs. 1:28-40). They move with dispatch, doing as David commanded. They put Solomon on David's mule as a public proclamation for all to see that Solomon is the successor to the throne. Next Solomon was anointed by Zadok the priest. This was in the tradition of Saul and David who were both anointed with oil as a sign of their call by God. Anointing symbolized God's favor and the endowment of the Spirit of God upon the king. So now Solomon would be seen as having a special son-like relationship with God.

Finally, the trumpet was sounded and all the people present for the anointing shouted, "Long live King Solomon!" (1 Kgs 1:39 NIV).

David's initiative to anoint Solomon king takes place during Adonijah's campaign dinner. As the feast concludes they hear the noise in the distant background. Without delay, Abiathar's son Jonathan arrives with the news that Solomon has been made king.

If that news was not enough to convince Adonijah that his plot was over, the story as it unfolds certainly would (1 Kgs. 1:41-53). For Jonathan says that the whole city resounded with cheering as Solomon arrived (1 Kgs. 1:45). It is clear that Solomon has the popular support so desired by politicians. He has taken his seat on the royal throne. His reign has begun. Only a bloody coup could reverse things now. Furthermore, the royal officials around David have thrown their support Solomon's way. The final confirmation for Adonijah and his supporters that Solomon is securely enthroned is the report of David's response. His full support is acted out on his sickbed as he bows in worship to thank God that he has been allowed to see his successor on the throne.

Having heard all that has happened, Adonijah's supporters quickly disperse. Adonijah himself fears for his life so much that he takes hold of the horns of the altar and begs Solomon for mercy (1 Kgs. 1:49-50). Solomon agrees not to harm Adonijah as long as he proves his worthiness—clearly meaning his loyalty to the throne. So Adonijah is given leave to go home.

The story of Solomon's ascension in the face of Adonijah's conspiracy highlights the grace of God. The one who put himself forward grasping for power is brought down while the one to whom the throne is promised, even though the youngest, is lifted up and seated on the throne. Clearly, power and the ability to rule are gifts from God.

The charge David gives to Solomon illustrates the covenant of grace upon which the throne is based. David calls Solomon to be strong and show himself to be a man (1 Kgs. 2:1-12). Yet the surprise comes in how David redefines what strength and manliness are all about. Surprisingly, he continues saying, " . . . observe what the Lord your

God requires: Walk in his ways, and keep his decrees and commands, his laws and requirements, as written in the Law of Moses, so that you may prosper in all that you do and wherever you go . . . " (1 Kgs. 2:3 NIV). Power and manliness come from living within God's covenant.

Summary

In the Bible the story of God's steadfast love is told and retold. Perhaps no other biblical story shows the mercy and grace of God better than the one of David. From the beginning David responded wholeheartedly to God by trying to walk in the ways of the Lord.

David, in all of his humanness, invites us into his life, and the gift we receive is to feel and to know God's great love for humankind. Even though David was deceptive, manipulative, and controlling in many of his encounters, he continued to be the recipient of God's forgiveness and mercy.

The significance of David's life goes on throughout the Bible. It is through the lineage of David that we are given God's Son, Jesus Christ, the One who comes to all persons with compassion, mercy, and love. This love is so encompassing and broad that each of us can know and experience what it means to be in a relationship of wholeness to God.

Discussion and Action

1. Reflect on the story in 1 Kings 1:1—2:12. Why did God choose David to be king? What has happened to David as he grows old?
2. Discuss the significance of Nathan's relationship with David. Be sure to include all the encounters between David and Nathan. Why is a prophetic voice (like Nathan's) important?
3. Having studied the life of David, how would you interpret the phrase "David—a man after the heart of God"? What is the meaning of David's life for you?
4. Discuss situations in your life and in the church where you see power and politics in action. Where are people "putting themselves forward" in order to gain power for themselves?
5. Take some time to share with one another the incident from David's life that impacted you the most and explain why.